Roman Soldier

Ba

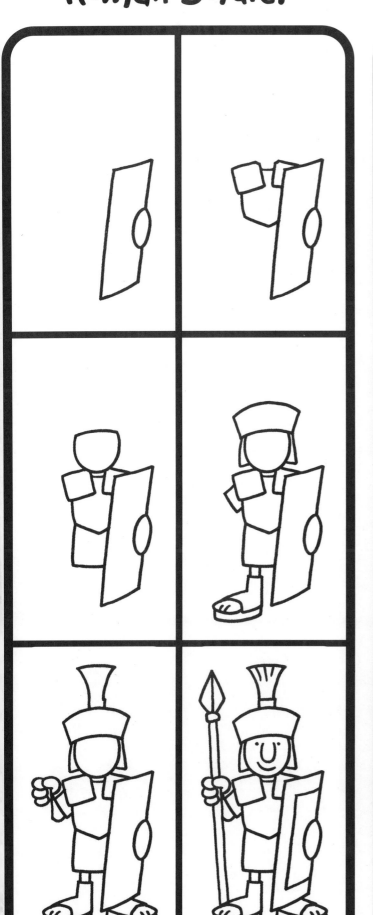

Roller Blades

Mechanic

Astronaut

School Girl

King

Queen

Doctor

African Musician

Mum

Dad

Brother

Sister

Gran   Grandad

Pharaoh   # Clown

Skateboarder   # Greek Scholar

Cowboy

Flamenco Dancer

Toddler

Judge

Greek Soldier

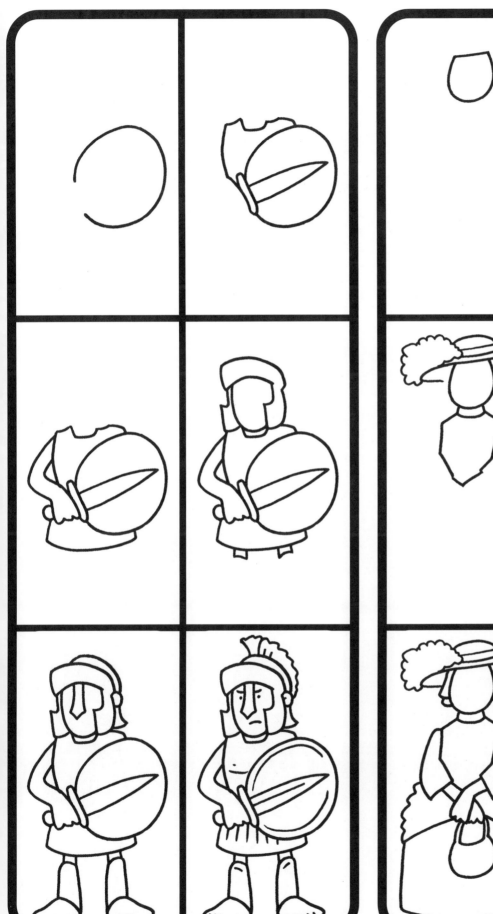

Victorian Lady

Teddy Boy   Teacher

Black Belt

Sailor

Tennis Player

Builder

Bride   # father christmas

Roman Emperor

Nurse

opera Singer

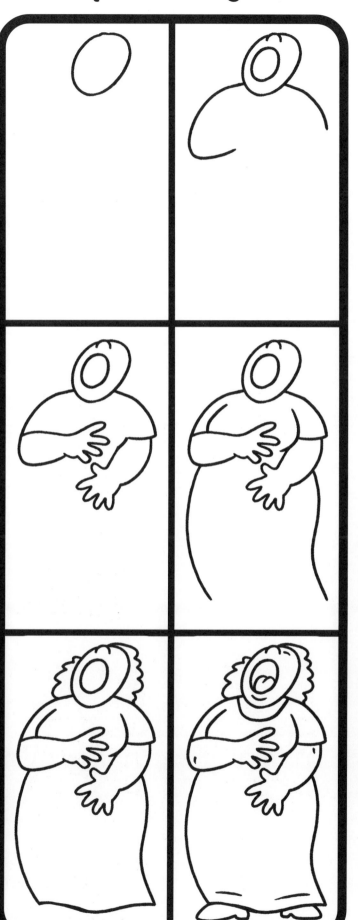

Sheriff

Artist

Witch

Dentist   Football Player

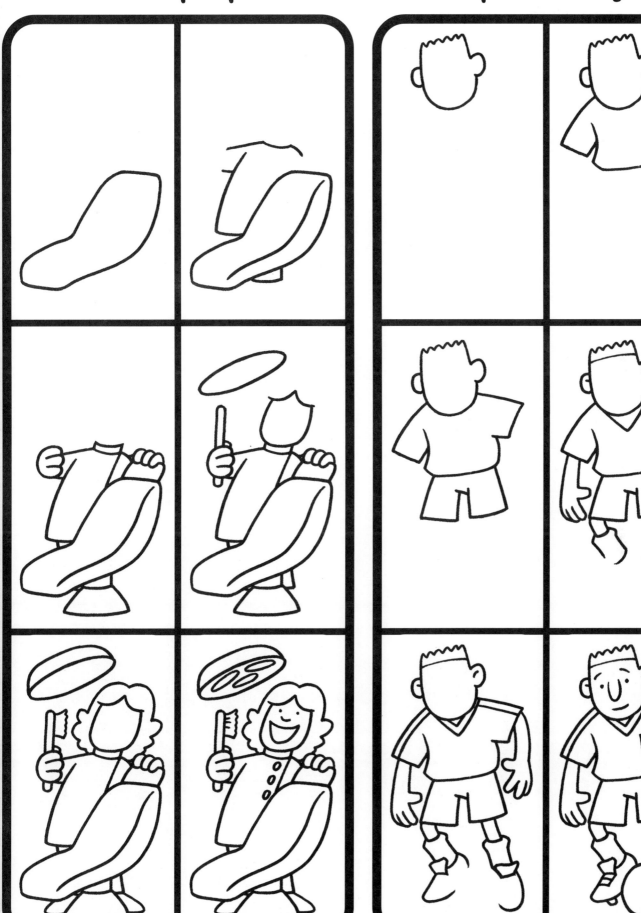

Ice Skater

Super Hero

Diver

Burglar

Chef

Elf

Cave Woman

Cave Man

Gardener

Baseball Player

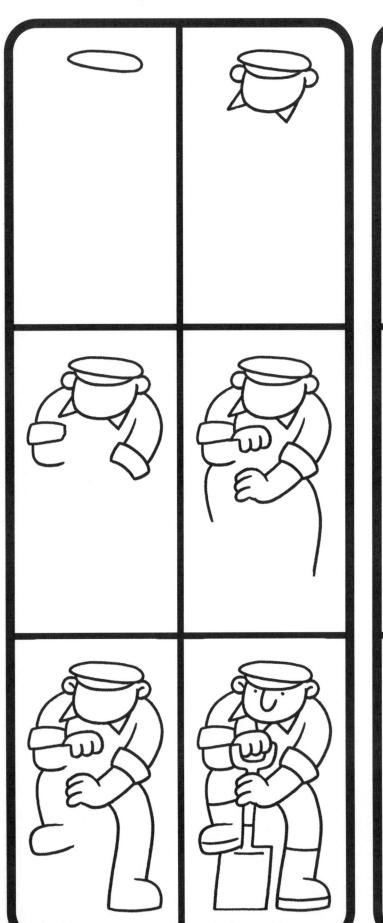

Fairy   Baker

Tightrope Walker   Fisherman

Magician   Knight

Policeman

BMX

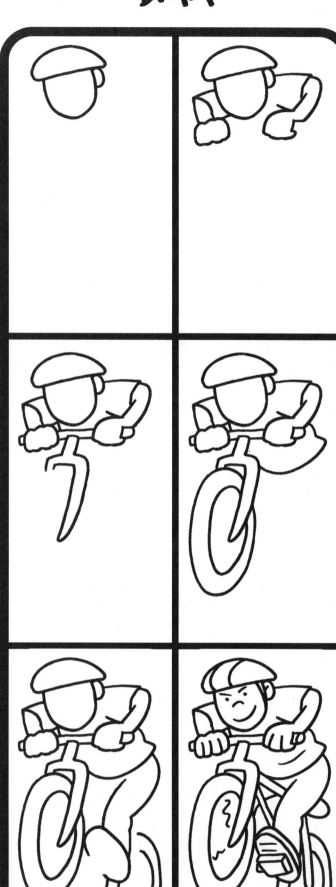

Rock'n'Roll Dancer

Postman

Eskimo   Scuba Diver

Fireman

Arab

Hippy   Lumberjack

Emperor
Indian Dancer

Victorian Gentleman

Ballet Dancer

Painter

farmer

Viking

Jump

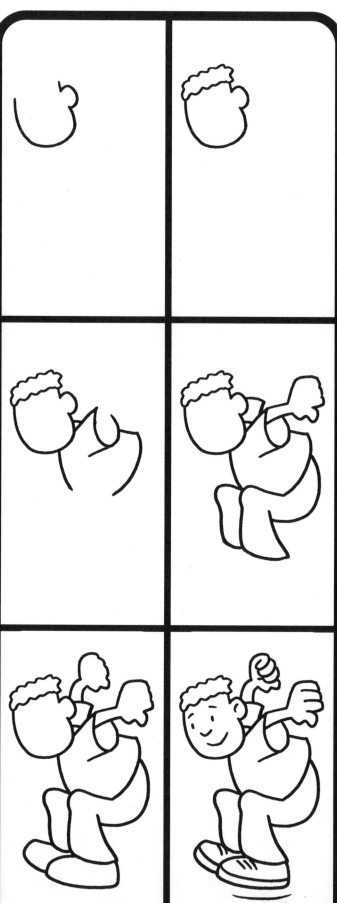

Skip

1970s Pop Star

Actor

Handstand

Surgeon

Chinese Lady

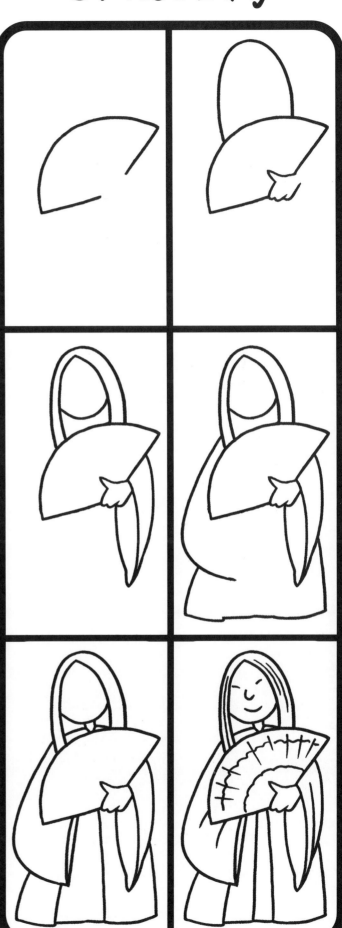

Scientist

Butcher

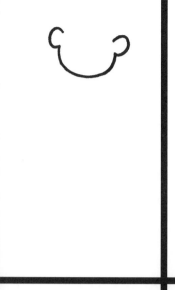

Pirate

Mountaineer

Deep Sea Diver

Wizard

Captain

Dwarf

Tarzan

Skier

Surfer

Vicar

High Jumper

Weightlifter

Juggler

conductor

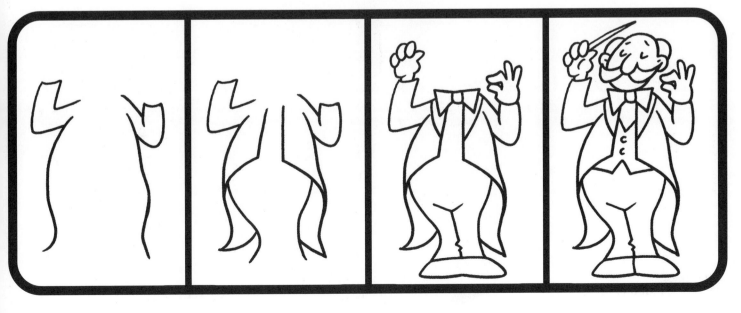

Basketball Player

Waiter

American football Player

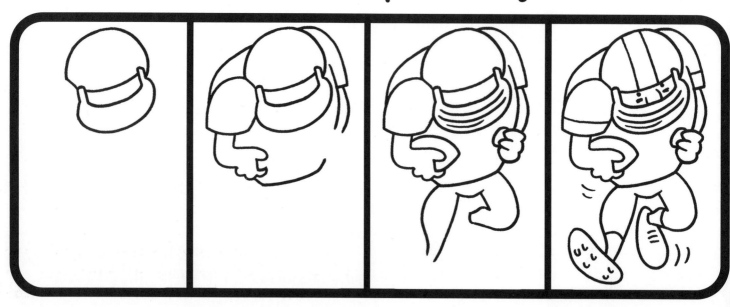